THE INDEPENDENT RECRUITER : 10 SIMPLE STEPS TO SUCCESS!

BY
Shiree
Alexander

LEARN STRATEGIES & MUST HAVE QUALITIES RECRUITERS
NEED TO SUCCEED!
BE THE GO-TO RECRUITER HIRING MANAGERS & CANDIDATES
LOVE TO WORK WITH!

SEARCH
JOB
DATA
SCREENING
ANALYSIS
RELAT
TALENT
RESUME
CONTRACT
REQUIREMENTS
PERSO
ANALYSIS
TALE
CANDIDATES
PROCES
ENCIES
TION
RECRUITMENT
EFITS
ONLINE
SALES
IZATIONS
CAREER
ILITY
NING
OFFER
WEBSITES
HELP
PROCESS

SHIREE ALEXANDER

The Independent Recruiter: 10 Simple Steps To Success!

Be the go-to recruiter hiring managers & candidates love to work with!

This book was professionally typeset on Reedsy.
Find out more at reedsy.com

Contents

Preface   v

I   Understanding What It Is To Be Independent

Closing & Full Cycle Recruiting   3

II   Candidates

Approach   7
Asking the Right Questions (Candidates)   9
Submitting Candidates   11
Feedback   13

III   Hiring Managers

Asking The Right Questions (Hiring Manager)   17
Challenges & Obstacles   19
What Do Hiring Managers Really Want?   21

IV   Congrats! Your Candidate Is Hired!

Your Candidate Is The Chosen One..Now What?   25

V   Sorry, Your Candidate Was Not Chosen

So...Your Candidate Wasn't Selected   29
Conclusion   31
About the Author   33
Also by Shiree Alexander   35

Preface

Do you love helping people? Have you always wanted to run your own small business as an independent recruiter? Are you a corporate recruiter ready to branch off on your own? This simple ten step guide will help you take action, and put you in the right mindset to do well in this business. If you are looking to achieve real success, this is for you.

I'm Shiree Alexander. I've worked in many roles from HR to Recruiting to Technology and much in between crossing over many industry sectors. I started this as a side hustle working my day job, and grew tired of the corporate politics.

My interest in this started years ago while in one of my first recruitment jobs. I was the person working with recruiting agencies, and saw the checks being cut to them. I thought why can't I do this... Oh, I'm already doing it just not getting paid for it?! Why should I be making $30K a year at a 'job' when I'm cutting someone else a check for $30K on ONE person!? I eventually just got to the point that I needed to do things my way, as I knew my was better. I'm great at what I do, and working in a corporate environment was a stifling creativity killer! I wanted to earn real money for the time and effort I was putting into making someone else rich. That led me to start my own Recruiting, Coaching, and Consulting company ExecuSane Inc.

I've placed well over 1,000 people during the course of my career. I've coached countless numbers of job seekers needing interview advice, and provided guidance to employees having issues in the workplace. Managers and small business owners have requested my services to help them in improving hiring & retention strategies, leadership, and managing conflict.

Thanks so much for your purchase of this booklet, and taking the initiative to learn & improve your skills. We need more great recruiters in this business.

-Shiree

I

Understanding What It Is To Be Independent

It takes drive, motivation, and a real desire to help people to succeed in this industry.

You have to play recruiter, coach, and consultant to help candidates and hiring managers through the process so that YOU get paid in the end.

1

Closing & Full Cycle Recruiting

Full cycle means that you have to be salesperson, marketer, sourcer, recruiter, closer, negotiator, consultant. YOU ARE THE TEAM.

You have to be able to close the deal on the front and back end. This means being a great salesperson to obtain the business... while also continuing to market/develop for new business... while also recruiting and placing candidates for your current clients.

There is no one else. You have to find the perfect balance to be successful in this business. As you grow and start earning income you can then choose to hire additional help, but until then roll up your sleeves and get to work!

II

Candidates

*How to approach and treat candidates to make a
lasting impression*

2

Approach

When first approaching a candidate to discuss a position please know what you're talking about!

Understand exactly what the job is to ensure you are targeting the right people. Know about the company and industry. Get all necessary details you need from the hiring manager so that you are presenting yourself in the best possible light to candidates.

Please know that not everyone is desperate for a job. Some people you're contacting are in high demand especially in highly skilled, or specialized areas. Some won't even return your calls, or respond to you. They get recruiters calling them all the time, and can go anywhere they choose. They get frustrated with multiple recruiters calling them that have no real knowledge of the position they are contacting them about. The least you can do is take the time out to fully understand the job, and have knowledge of the industry you're recruiting in so you can better connect with your target market. Be prepared.

You are being judged as well. You are the face of your company, and your reputation is on the line. You need to not only make yourself look good, but also fully be able to represent the client you are working with.

3

Asking the Right Questions (Candidates)

If a candidate calls YOU:

If a candidate calls you based on a job you've put out there you'd tell them about the role, and ask questions to assess if they are a fit. Have them send over their resume. Ask questions such as what type of role are you seeking? What industries interest you most? What would you want in the next role that you may not have gotten in your previous? Have a preference for a small or large company? Prefer working on a team or independent? Salary range etc? They called you so the objective is to get a feel for them to see if they're a good fit for your current client, or any others you have in the loop.

If YOU call them it takes on a different path:

First, make sure they are open to speaking about your opportunity as they may not be interested. Give them all information pertaining to the position, and be certain they understand. Then, start asking questions pertaining to how their experience matches the job you have available. So how do you feel your experience matches this role? Explain more to me about your background & what salary you'd be seeking for a role like this etc.

Make sure you get a full understanding of the candidate's background and experience so you are submitting the right type of people. Don't just send hiring managers anything?! Remember, quality over quantity.

4

Submitting Candidates

When submitting a candidate make sure you know how to sell them! This could be the difference between you getting paid or not. Don't let a misunderstanding, or not being knowledgeable enough about the job hinder you from your goals.

A recruiter that cannot properly sell a candidate not only hurts themselves, but could prevent a well deserving person from getting a job.

This is why understanding, and having the correct job description is so important. You and the hiring manager need to be on the same page. Be certain to clarify everything to make sure nothing is missed as far as the the candidate's experience & background. Learn everything about the candidate, and any transferrable skills that may be valuable to the job. Talk them up, and sell their skills like your life depends on it.

There was once a time a candidate I was working with had one small thing lacking on their resume that was crucial to the job, and they were up against major competition. I knew this person was perfect for the job, but wasn't relaying all their info properly. The manager really liked this person, but hung up on this one small thing they felt was lacking. I dug a bit deeper, and listened to the manager's concerns. I went back and clarified those concerns with the candidate in which they informed me they had that exact experience, but due to another recruiter telling them to shorten their resume they'd left it off!!! I told them to send me a separate write up specific to what my client was asking for, and explain how their experience directly related. This sealed the deal, and my candidate got the job!

It 'almost' didn't happen. There was another person the manager felt was a better fit at first, but they liked my candidate's personality best. I knew I had to get this person across the finish line, and I did!

$$$ Ten Grand In My Hand! $$$

5

Feedback

Always give feedback throughout the process even if your candidate doesn't get the job. Respect people's time. Don't leave anyone hanging. The staffing & recruiting industry is known for doing this. Do not be one of those recruiters that treat people like they're just another number. Be respectful of them as people, and value their time.

It's hard work looking for a job. Looking for a job is a job within itself. People have lives, families, bills to pay... You don't know what they are going through. Please consider this, and understand that they are taking their time engaging with you in hopes that you can help them in some way.

Their interaction with you could potentially change their lives for the better. That's serious to think about, and it's discouraging to consistently be rejected and have to keep your head up in the process. Most people are rejected multiple times before landing a job offer. Please think about the impact you have on others. Keep it courteous, and keep it positive.

That candidate you don't place today could be the same candidate you do place tomorrow!

Treat them the way you'd like to be treated!

III

Hiring Managers

How to ask the right questions & overcome challenges

6

Asking The Right Questions (Hiring Manager)

Get all details of the position from the hiring manager. Help them balance their priorities for the role. Make them see the difference between the wants vs needs. This is where you put on your coach/consulting hat. Help them to help you! You get paid if you make a placement!

They sometimes think they know what they want and need, and expectations can be unrealistic. You don't want to spin your wheels looking for the wrong person, or someone that doesn't exist!

A few examples of things to ask a hiring manager include:
What is the job title?
What do you truly need? Are you needing someone more junior, mid, or senior level?
Why is the position open- Is it a new role or is someone leaving?
What are the daily challenges?

Work hours? Is it a standard 8 hour shift or is overtime the norm?

Any remote or flex time schedules?

Any travel involved?

Open to relocate someone?

Who does it report to?

What are your short and long term expectations/goals for this position?

Make sure you get all pertinent information so that you are targeting the right people. Wasted time running after the wrong person also prevents the right person from being discovered. They may have stopped looking, or possibly taken by another company.

Time is money! Don't waste it!

7

Challenges & Obstacles

There are times in which you may experience pushback from hiring managers. Some just want to do things their way which makes your job more difficult. They don't understand the importance of having a detailed job description that attracts exactly the kind of candidate they need. They'll throw you a little of nothing, and expect you to find the best person. Or, they go too far with an unrealistic expectation that results in no one and wonder why they aren't getting results.

You have to educate them on what needs to be done, and WHY it needs to be done. Whether its adding to, or tweaking the job description to make some improvement. Maybe their company reputation isn't the best, and they need help in branding their company as the place people want to be a part of. Figure out how you can help them see that, and find a way to include that in your marketing strategy when looking for candidates. What makes this company stand out above the others? What perks could they offer that would really make them competitive? This is also a place to act as consultant. Remember, if you are helping them with these type of initiatives the more tasks you take on the more you need to consider charging for additional services. They are supposed to have all this figured out at the point they engage you to help in filling their position. It's OK to coach them a bit, but if you start helping a company with their overall branding strategy, and revamping or totally creating job descriptions from scratch you may need to charge extra for your value added services :)

There may be times you have to walk away. If it's too difficult to get them to see things rationally then you end up wasting a lot of valuable time. You want to work with clients that get it, value their people, and want the best for everyone involved.

8

What Do Hiring Managers Really Want?

The best managers want the best people filling their roles.

They want the best recruiters working alongside them.

They are looking for top quality candidates.

They want transparency on how the process is going.

They want feedback on what's working and whats not.

If something isn't working they want help in seeing what will.

Help guide them through the process so it's a win win for everyone.

It's that simple.

IV

Congrats! Your Candidate Is Hired!

9

Your Candidate Is The Chosen One..Now What?

Congrats! Get with your client to discuss salary, start date, background checks etc..

Have them send you the job offer in writing. Contact your candidate, and give them the great news! Send the offer over, and inform them that it's contingent upon passing all necessary pre-employment screening (whatever is required by the company).

Make sure that they are comfortable with the salary offered, and anything else that is stated in the offer letter. If not take the concerns back to the hiring manager, and see what needs to be done so that everyone is in agreement.

Help them through any further questions, or concerns they may have. Count down the days to their start date, and your pay date :) On the day they officially start the job check in with you client be sure they arrived on time, and see how their first day is going.

Call the candidate after their first shift is over, and ask how their day went. You want to find out about the job, how they were treated etc...

Promptly send your invoice over to the client on day 1 of the candidates start date! Make sure your invoice has the same payment terms listed in your contract (net 30 or net 15) or whatever agreement you all have.

Keep checking in periodically especially in the beginning with both the client and candidate to see how they're doing, and make sure all is well.

V

Sorry, Your Candidate Was Not Chosen

10

So...Your Candidate Wasn't Selected

Ask the hiring manager for feedback. Get specifics as to why your candidate wasn't selected so that you can relay that info back to them. Thank your candidate for the opportunity to work with them, and let them know you will keep them in mind for future opportunities. Thank the hiring manager for allowing you to work with them as well.

Now, the next question is did your client fill the role with someone else, or is the role still open but your candidate just wasn't a fit for them? This means you may still have an opportunity to fill the position if you've submitted more than one person.

Otherwise, if the client has filled the job do not let it frustrate you too much. Keep it moving...

Remember, you were supposed to continuously be focused on marketing at all times while recruiting for current clients.

Always be developing new business to keep a pipeline going. That way when one thing doesn't work out you're not right back at square one.

You're in it to win it!

11

Conclusion

Please do the best you can for candidates, clients, and most importantly yourself!

You are in this business to help others, and make money in the process.

Don't make the mistake of thinking this is **all** about money. You're definitely in for that, but you need to have true passion for helping others to achieve long term success .

You have the ability to change lives.

Making a placement gives people a way to make a living including YOU!

Take pride in what you do, and be the best at it!

Thank You!

-Shiree Alexander

Want more insight? Sign up today *for the online course that compliments this 10 Step booklet!*

*This eBook already comes packaged with the course so I've **discounted the course by 15%** as a thank you for your book purchase ! **Just enter code 15PERCENTOFF at checkout.***

About the Author

Hi,

I'm Shiree Alexander.

Mom, Wife, and a million other titles...

I own ExecuSane Inc Recruitment, Coaching, and Consulting company based in Dallas, TX. I assist businesses with their recruitment needs, and offer coaching/consulting services in hiring & retention, leadership, and conflict resolution.

I'm also a career coach focused on guiding job seekers through the interview process, and helping those already employed with issues affecting them in the workplace.

My background spans multiple industries from HR/Recruitment, Technology, Real Estate, Healthcare, and more. I love helping people in whatever way I can, and enjoy helping businesses especially small growing ones hire and retain the best talent and leadership to keep them moving forward.

You can connect with me on:

🌐 https://execusane.com

Also by Shiree Alexander

The Beginner's Guide To Starting A Profitable Home Based Recruiting Business!
Earn thousands of dollars per placement working from home or anywhere you choose! Ditch the 9-5 & join the world of independent recruiting!

www.ingramcontent.com/pod-product-compliance
Lightning Source LLC
Chambersburg PA
CBHW020713180526
45163CB00008B/3074